A TO B

by Tia-Renee Mullings

Produced by JFR Productions in association with Soho Theatre and HighTide Theatre, *A to B*, directed by Ewa Dina, was first performed on 12 June 2026 at Soho Theatre, London.

CAST

Amani	Sheyi Cole
Brianna	Zakiyyah Deen

CREATIVES

Director	Ewa Dina
Producer	Jasmyn Fisher-Ryner (for JFR Productions)
Associate Producer	Suher Sofi
Set & Costume Designer	Sange Falase
Lighting Designer	Cheng Keng
Sound Designer & Composer	Khalil Madovi
Movement Director	Jade Hackett
Production Manager	Herbe Walmsley
Dramaturg	Titilola Dawudu
Stage Manager	Danielle Adéyínka-Uchè
Stage Manager	Joshua Cole-Brown
Cover Photography	Courtney Nathan Phillip
Post Production Edit	David Oldenburg
Marketing	Mobius Industries
PR	Oliva O'Neill (for Chloé Nelkin Consulting)

JFR Productions would like to thank Hackney Empire, Soho Walthamstow and Oliver Brown

CAST

Sheyi Cole | Amani

Sheyi most recently starred in Steven Soderbergh's *Full Circle* on HBO Max and in Chichester Festival Theatre's *Lord of the Flies*. His first screen role was as the title role in Steve McQueen's stand-alone film *Alex Wheatle*, in his multi-award-winning *Small Axe* anthology for BBC and Amazon.

Previous credits include a guest lead in the Emmy and Golden Globe-winning *Atlanta* (FX/Disney+), the Netflix feature *The Homeless World Cup* and the BFI Film/FIlm4 feature *Boxing Day*. Sheyi was selected as one of Screen International's Stars of Tomorrow 2020. He's made numerous 'rising stars' lists since then, and was recently named one of 'Forbes 30 Under 30' in the entertainment sphere; the prestigious Dazed100 Hot List 2023 and nominated by John Boyega for the Gen Now Award at the inaugural Soho House Awards.

Zakiyyah Deen | Brianna

Zakiyyah is an actor and writer born and bred in London with Afro-Caribbean roots. She was selected as one of only four writers out of six hundred for the NFTS x Left Bank Pictures Diverse Writers Development Programme 2025, where she developed original scripted ideas, led and partook in writers' rooms and worked closely with industry mentors.

Zakiyyah debuted her full-length play, *Why a Black Woman Will Never Be Prime Minister*, at Camden People's Theatre, where she took on the roles of writer, lead actor, and co-producer. The play received critical acclaim and a sold-out three-week run. It has recently been shortlisted for the prestigious Mustapha Matura Award and Mentoring Programme.

Other credits include *Brassic FM* (The Gate Theatre) and *Is Dat U Yh?* (Brixton House). Zakiyyah also starred in the lead role in the Netflix-funded short, *The Journey of Self*. She has collaborated with Academy Award-winning director Steve McQueen on his anthology series *Small Axe* and played a series regular in the BBC Three series *Enterprice*, created by Kayode Ewumi.

Zakiyyah was Theatre Deli's Classic Residency Artist in 2022 and Tara Theatre's Constellations Artist in 2023.

CREATIVE TEAM

Tia-Renee Mullings | Writer

Tia-Renee Mullings is a South London-born and raised British-Caribbean writer and spoken word poet. She won the Mustapha Matura Award (2023) for her first play *Little Angela Davis*, which was also shortlisted for the Alfred Fagon Award. Her second play, *A to B* (shortlisted for the Women's Prize for Playwriting) received two readings at the Royal Court Theatre before being presented as a Shedinburgh Original at the Edinburgh Fringe 2025. Her play *Duppies* was performed as part of the Royal Court Open Submissions Festival in 2026. As a poet, Tia-Renee has headlined CLiCK Poetry Festival and Zenith Poetry, and performed on BBC Radio London. She is an alumnus of the Royal Court's Introductory writers' group 2024 and is currently part of the Channel 4Screenwriting 2026 cohort. *A to B*, which runs at Soho Theatre in June 2026, is her debut play.

Ewa Dina | Director

Ewa is a Nigerian-born, Sheffield-raised, and London-based director, actor, facilitator, and poet. Since graduating from Rose Bruford, she has built a multidisciplinary practice across theatre and performance.

Music and movement are central to her work, shaping how stories are told and experienced. She creates work that expands our understanding of ourselves, encourages discourse, and leads rooms with compassion, collaboration, and openness.

She is the winner of the 2026 JMK Award.

Recent credits include: *The Welsh Dragon* (Theatre Iolo); *Her Naked Skin* (Rose Bruford); *The Kola Nut Does Not Speak English* (Bush Theatre); *No More Mr Nice Guy* (Original Director – R&D, Camden People's Theatre).

Assistant and associate credits include: Resident Assistant Director, Donmar Warehouse (2025–2026): *Dealer's Choice* (Matthew Dunster), *Intimate Apparel* (Lynette Linton), *The Maids* (Kip Williams), *When We Are Married* (Tim Sheader).

Resident Director: *TINA: The Tina Turner Musical* (2024–2025).

Associate Director: Regent's Park Open Air Theatre: *Every Leaf a Hallelujah* (Chinonyerem Odima).

More information at ewadina.com

Jasmyn Fisher-Ryner | Producer for JFR Productions

Jasmyn Fisher-Ryner is a two-time Olivier-nominated, award-winning theatre producer known for her work on critically acclaimed productions across the UK and West End. She is an independent theatre and digital producer, and events and outreach consultant from East London. She is the company director for her production company JFR Productions Ltd. She worked as a producer for the Royal Court Theatre and was nominated for the Best Producer Award at the Black British Theatre Awards in 2022 for producing and platforming the production of *For Black Boys Who Have Considered Suicide When The Hue Gets Too Heavy* at the Royal Court Theatre. Jasmyn's work spans across other London theatre and the West End with a strong focus on working for and with different community and young people groups.

She's dedicated to platforming emerging artists in spaces that celebrate diversity, accessibility and radical change within theatre and entertainment.

As a theatre producer, Jasmyn produced the award-winning Edinburgh show *Eat The Rich (but maybe not me mates x)* by Jade Franks and was selected for the competitive Stage One 5 to 50 scheme, mentored by Francesca Moody. Her producing credits include the double Olivier-nominated *For Black Boys Who Have Considered Suicide When the Hue Gets Too Heavy* by Ryan Calais Cameron (Royal Court Theatre, 2022/Apollo Theatre, 2023/Garrick Theatre, 2024) and the Olivier-nominated *Blue Mist* (Royal Court Theatre, 2023). As an Associate Producer, she worked on *Why A Black Woman Will Never Be Prime Minister* (Camden People's Theatre, 2024).

Alongside this, Jasmyn is a digital producer, managing and producing the *Frame of Mind* podcast.

Jasmyn is the Producing Events Consultant for Central School of Speech and Drama.

Jasmyn is on the board of trustees for the Hackney Empire.

Suher Sofi | Associate Producer

Suher Sofi is a British Somali producer and filmmaker, and the founder of JanFirst Productions. Driven by a passion for amplifying diverse voices and stories, she works across TV, film, and theatre. She has produced multiple sold-out productions, including *Desperate Times* (Pleasance Theatre, 2024/ Birmingham Hippodrome, 2024/Liverpool Unity Theatre, 2024/Bristol Old Vic, 2024) and *Crush* (Soho Theatre, 2026), which was featured in *British Vogue*.

Alongside her theatre work, Suher has built television credits on programmes including *The One Show*, *Educating Yorkshire*, *Amol Rajan Interviews*, and *Life & Death Row*. In 2025, she made her documentary directorial debut with *Untold Stories Part 2*, which was selected for the African Film Festival Atlanta 2026. She was also selected for Stage One's Bridge the Gap programme for 2025–26.

Sange Falase | Set & Costume Designer

Sange is an interdisciplinary spatial artist, performance designer and writer based in London, working within theatre, screen and installation.

They have a keen interest in integrating speculative spatial design methodologies as a tool for envisioning liberatory futures. They were part of the Soho Theatre Writers Lab cohort from 2024 to 2025.

Theatre credits include: *ADP 2025* (Hackney Empire); *TYPT 2023* and *2024* (Talawa Theatre Company); *Brassic FM* (Gate Theatre, London); *Sucker Punch* (Queen's Theatre Hornchurch/UK tour); *J'Ouvert* (Theatre503/Sonia Friedman Productions); *This is Black* (Bunker Theatre); *Romeo and Juliet* (Orange Tree Theatre); *Living Newspaper* (Royal Court); *Family Tree* (ATC Theatre/GDIF); *Emilia* (LAMDA); *Passion Fruit* (New Diorama); *The Mountaintop* (UK tour).

Film includes: *This Love Isn't Taught* (BFI Flare/Euras Films); *Signs* (BFI) and *Brain in Gear* (BBC).

Associate and assistant design credits include: *A Small Place* (Gate Theatre); *The Long Song* (Chichester Festival Theatre); *The Tempest* (Shakespeare's Globe).

Sange has worked on various exhibitions across venues that include the ICA, TATE and Afropunk 2018.

Cheng Keng | Lighting Designer

Cheng Keng is a scenographer, lighting and video designer based in London. He trained at Royal Central School of Speech and Drama, completing an MFA in Scenography.

Theatre credits include: *Welcome to Pemfort* (Soho Theatre); *tell me straight / aggy, Going for Gold* (Park Theatre); *Loop, Bungalow* (Theatre503); *The Quiz, Frankenstein, Rain Weaver, 1984* (Cockpit Theatre); *Poetess* (Pleasance Jack Dome); *Testament, 555: Verlaine En Prison, At the Statue of Venus / La Voix humaine* (Arcola Theatre); *Riders to the Sea* (MAST); *The Light Princess* (The ARC); *The Lonesome Death of Eng Bunker, Tiger* (Omnibus); *Grud* (Hampstead Theatre); *Grills, Project Atom Boi, So That You May Go Beyond The Sea* (Camden People's Theatre); *1884* (Shoreditch Town Hall); *The Littlest Yak* (Marlowe Studio); *Chriskirkpatrickmas* (Seven Dials Playhouse); *Let Your Hands Sing In The Silence* (Marlowe Theatre); *These Words That'll Linger Like Ghosts Till The Day I Drop Down Dead* (The Pleasance); *The Retreat, Pennyroyal* (Finborough Theatre); *The Zone* (Taoyuan Art Centre); *Sankofa: Before the Whitewash* (Roundhouse); *Beauty and the 7 Beasts* (Brixton Jamm); *Borders* (Drayton Arms Theatre); *Blue Island 99* (International Dublin Gay Theatre Festival); *Hello World* (National Taichung Theatre, Taiwan).

Khalil Madovi | Sound Designer & Composer

Khalil is an award-winning music artist, composer, writer, actor and filmmaker. In 2024 Khalil was nominated for a Black British Theatre Award for his sound design work and received an OFFIE nomination for Best Sound Design for *Red Pitch*. Khalil has most recently performed in Chadwick Boseman's *Deep Azure* at the Globe.

Theatre work as sound designer includes: *Julius Caesar* (Tangle Theatre); *The Two Gentlemen of Verona* (RSC); *Why a Black Woman Will Never Be Prime Minister* (Camden People's Theatre); *G* (Royal Court); *Red Pitch* (Bush Theatre/Soho Place); *No More Mr. Nice Guy* (Broadway Theatre, Catford/UK tour); *Brenda's Got a Baby* (New Diorama); *Metamorphoses* (RADA); *Divine* (Arts Ed); *This is What the Journey Does* (Old Vic, as part of One Voice: HOME series); *The Poison Belt* (Jermyn Street).

Work as composer and sound designer includes: *Fatherland* (Hampstead Theatre); *The Boy With Wings* (Polka Theatre/Birmingham Rep); *Animal Farm* (Theatre Royal Stratford East/Leeds Playhouse/Nottingham Playhouse); *Revealed* (Belgrade Theatre, Coventry/Tobacco Factory); *Gone Too Far!* (Theatre Royal Stratford East); *Sound Clash: Death in the Arena* (Pleasance One, Edinburgh Fringe); *Can I Live?* (Barbican).

Jade Hackett | Movement Director

With more than twenty years within the hip-hop dance industry and over ten years within the theatre industry, Jade has become a seasoned movement storyteller specialising in creating work solely designed to connect and move audiences with relatable and thought provoking narratives. Having worked across theatre, television and film, Jade's artistic voice gravitates to a cinematic style. This particular project is not 100% dance or theatre. It's somewhere in the middle that aims to provide a new way of consuming real stories of the heart.

Her credits include the following: theatre as performer includes: *Sylvia* (The Old Vic); *Nine Night, Into Da Hoodz: Remixed, Some Like It HipHop* (West End); *Pied Piper* (Barbican); *The Mad Hatter's Tea Party* (Roundhouse/Royal Opera House); *A Monster Calls* (Bristol Old Vic).

Theatre as choreographer includes: *Little Shop of Horrors, Miss Saigon* (Sheffield Crucible); *Hex* (National Theatre).

Theatre as associate choreographer: *For Black Boys Who Have Considered Suicide When The Hue Gets Too Heavy* (Apollo Theatre); *Sylvia* (Old Vic); *CYCLES* (Barbican/Lincoln Centre).

Theatre as associate choreographer/co-associate director includes: *Get Up Stand Up! The Bob Marley Musical* (West End).

Theatre as movement director includes: *Titus Andronicus* (RSC); *Reverberation* (Bristol Old Vic); *White Noise* (Bridge Theatre); *The Tempest* (Arcola Theatre).

Theatre as director and choreographer includes: *The Tide* (Talawa).

Theatre as assistant movement director: *For Black Boys Who Have Considered Suicide When the Hue Gets Too Heavy* (Royal Court); UK choreographer: *Slave Play* (Noël Coward Theatre).

Associate director: *Once Flew Over the Cuckoo's Nest* (Old Vic).

Television choreographer credits: *Mr Loverman* (BBC); *Dreaming Whilst Black* (BBC3/Disney+).

Herbe Walmsley | Production Manager

Herbe Walmsley is a production manager & sound designer.

Production management credits include: *Dear Jack, Dear Louise* (Arcola Theatre); *My Brother's a Genius, Dizzy* (Sheffield Playhouse); *Count Dykula* (Soho Theatre); *Derry Boys, Bungalow* (Theatre503); *Going for Gold* (Daphne Hackett Theatre Barbados); *Lucy & Friends and Talawa Firsts on Tour.*

Sound design and sound associate credits include: *Answering Machines* (East Riding Theatre); *My Brother's a Genius* (Sheffield Playhouse).

Titilola Dawudu | Dramaturg

Titilola Dawudu the Artistic Director and CEO of HighTide. She is a dramaturg and writer whose work spans artist and writer development, literary and programming. Titilola most recently served as Associate Dramaturg at the Bush Theatre, where she led the literary department.

She co-created and edited *Hear Me Now: Audition Monologues for Actors of Colour* and as a playwright, Titilola's work has been staged at Theatre Peckham, Ovalhouse, Soho Theatre, Beyond Face and Theatre Royal Arojah, in Abuja, Nigeria. Her dramaturgical work includes *Shifters* by Benedict Lombe, alongside Deidre O'Halloran, and the Olivier-nominated *Miss Myrtle's Garden,* by Danny James King.

Danielle Adéyínka-Uchè | Stage Manager

Danielle Adéyínká-Uchè is an Olivier Award-winning stage manager and multidisciplinary creative based in London, working across theatre, live entertainment, music and cultural events. Their credits include productions such as *Small Island, Hey Duggee* and *Why a Black Woman Will Never Be Prime Minister,* alongside work across the West End, new writing and touring productions. Passionate about collaboration and community-led storytelling, Danielle blends creative operations, production and artistry to help bring bold, memorable experiences to life.

Joshua Cole-Brown | Stage Manager

Joshua Cole-Brown is a London-based stage manager and promoter rep working across theatre and live music. A graduate of the BRIT School and Guildhall School of Music & Drama (Production Arts), he brings a calm, collaborative presence and meticulous organisational flair to every project, from new writing, plays and musicals up to arena-scale concerts. He is a proud Londoner with Jamaican Heritage and looks forward to being part of the team on *A to B*.

Theatre credits span West End, touring and regional productions. Examples include: *Liberation* (Royal Exchange Theeatre, Manchester; directed by Monique Touko and written by Ntombizodwa Nyoni); *All My Sons* (Wyndham's Theatre; directed by Ivo Van Hove); *MJ The Musical* (Prince Edward Theatre; choreographed by Christopher Wheeldon); *Sunset Boulevard* (Savoy Theatre; directed by Jamie Lloyd).

In live music, Joshua serves as a versatile stage manager and promoter rep across gig venues, arenas, and outdoor festival stages. He has advanced and delivered shows for national tours, managed multi-band changeovers, coordinated backline and RF, and maintained seamless liaison between artists, promoters, and venues. Experience includes: End of the Road 2022–2026, All Points East 2024–2026, BST Hyde Park 2022–2026, Recessland, Henley Festival, The Other Songs Live for The Brit School at London Palladium & Provenance Sault, Chronixx, Cleo Sol For All Points East 2025.

Training: The BRIT School; Guildhall School of Music & Drama (Production Arts). Areas: Stage Management (book/deck), Show Calling, Promoter Rep/Admin, Artist Liaison, RF/Comms, Backline Coordination, Scheduling, Advance & Logistics.

PRODUCERS

JFR PRODUCTIONS

JFR Productions (JFRP) is a multifaceted production company dedicated to crafting moments and cultivating stories through theatrical, event consultancy and digital management.

We are committed to the journey that starts from a passing thought into a fully executed production. Ensuring that all work is accessible and available to all cultures and communities to experience. Because wh should anything be gate-kept?!

JFRP produces and invests in a range of work that focuses on underrepresented stories and storytelling through our theatre strand and produces and consults on impactful and meaningful events. The digital element of the company supports on producing content that provides a platform for people discuss topics close to their hearts.

We blend imagination with precision to bring your visions to life!

Email: Hello@jfrproduction.com
Website: jfrproduction.com
Facebook: JFR Productions

SOHO THEATRE

Soho Theatre is London's most vibrant producer for new theatre, comedy and cabaret. In 2025, our venue in Soho, central London, celebrated 25 years as one of the UK's busiest with a buzzing bar, lively audiences and an entertaining year-round festival programme with a queer, punk, counter-culture flavour. Our second London venue, Soho Theatre Walthamstow, opened in May 2025, bringing our vibrant programme to its biggest stage yet. Work extends beyond our venues with a full touring programme and connections with New York, Melbourne and Mumbai.

Edinburgh Festival Fringe is a huge part of our year; we present many shows and scout hundreds more and we are the UK's leading presenter of comedians from India. Our filmed comedy specials can be seen on international airlines and online and our artist development and participation programmes are as important as the work on our stages.

Soho Theatre is a charitably-owned social enterprise; with annual audiences projected to increase to over 400,000 in 2025, turnover to exceed £11m and strong international links, it makes a positive contribution to growth in creative industries and UK soft power.

HIGHTIDE THEATRE

HighTide is a writer-centred theatre company, based in the East of England. We produce new plays by playwrights from our region, touring across the East and beyond. We run a year-round writer development programme that creates space for East of England playwrights to thrive. We offer creative writing programmes in schools and community groups to build confidence, wellbeing and employability. We are committed to ensuring everyone, from all backgrounds, can participate in the joy and power of theatre. We believe that partnership and collaboration makes better theatre, as well as more lasting, positive social change. HighTide holds the climate crisis in its name; a daily reminder of our responsibility to act now – with imagination and creativity. We see climate and social justice as inextricably linked and believe that theatre can help rehearse a better future for us all.

HighTide's work is made possible by public investment in the arts from Arts Council England.

Principal Partner: Lansons | Team Farner

HighTide: 01473 459200 / hello@hightide.org.uk
Website | hightide.org.uk/
Facebook | HighTideTheatre
Twitter | @_HighTide_

A TO B

Tia-Renee Mullings

Acknowledgements

Thank you to Gill Greer and the Royal Court Theatre team.

Thank you to Darren Raymond and Intermission Youth Theatre.

Thank you to Francesca Moody Productions.

Thank you to Roy Alexander Weise, Tobi King Bakare, and Déja J. Bowens.

Thank you to Ewa Dina, Jasmyn Fisher-Ryner, Suher Sofi, and the rest of the creative and production team.

Thank you to Sheyi Cole and Zakiyyah Deen.

Thank you to my parents, my people dem, to Nova, Bunnie, and Shadow.

Big up JA and big up South East London.

T-R.M.

Characters

AMANI, *Black. Early twenties*
BRIANNA, *Black. Early twenties*

Both characters speak in BBE (Black British English)/MLE (Multicultural London English) and code-switch into Jamaican patois, as well as embodying other characters who speak in similar registers and riddims.

Notes on Text

(–) at the end of a line indicates an interruption/cut-off.

(–) by itself indicates a breath or a break in time.

(/) indicates lines spoken at the same time.

(***) indicates a new scene.

Notes on Performance

This play is written for two actors in the roles of Amani and Brianna. Actors should deploy the use of accents, body language, etc. to fully embody and distinguish between other characters.

Rhythm is the primary language of this play. Amani and Brianna's world is scored by the sounds of South London and the Caribbean – particularly Jamaica – and the soundscape should move with the characters emotionally and physically. Dancehall, reggae, grime, dub, lovers rock, and soca should punctuate, frame, and carry transitions between scenes.

The same sense of music and rhythm should inform how the lines are delivered, landing closer to spoken word poetry than strict naturalism.

Amani and Brianna's journeys happen concurrently. They move in and out of each other's spaces, stories, unaware. Sometimes there's a barrier, sometimes there isn't.

This text went to press before the end of rehearsals and so may differ slightly from the play as performed.

AMANI *springs into life.*

AMANI I wake up like a man on a mission.
A man
On a mission
To look as LENG as humanly possible
To impress a girl
That he's never met
That he's gonna meet…
Today!

Beat.

Naturally,
On account of being
This thing called
Black…
I don't gotta do too much.
The leng-ness comes pre-installed.
Pre-loaded.
Pre-arranged…
Especially in these summer months
Where you might as well call the sun a waiter…
With the way that it's been serving
Me
And my skin.
But today's different
Special
Important
So it can't be no 'moisturise and go' ting.

A phone alarm sounds, and BRIANNA *tries her best.*

BRIANNA I wake up like a woman on a mission.
A woman
On a mission
To go RIGHT back to sleep!

Her snooze alarm goes off again.

I wake up.
(*Yawning.*)
For real this time!
And roll over with a yawn and a stretch to find
that
To my HORROR
I'm making direct eye contact with my bonnet

BRIANNA *frantically touches the top of her head,*
sighs.

What a way to start the day, huh.
THE day.
The day that you've been
high-key
DREADING
Ever since you agreed to it…
Maybe
Possibly
The ONLY day
Where you actually need to look
Kind of decent…
No!
Where you actually need to look better than
you've EVER looked.
Because when you're dealing with matters of the
heart –
You have to be smart
And I got like three A-stars
So
I'm more than qualified…
Yeah.

Beat.

Okay I lied
'Cause I do better with plans
And less good with 'vibes'
Like, if there was a guide
To this stuff
I'd be ABSOLUTELY fine

But if I mess this up,
I'll be replaying it for the next three to five –

AMANI   I open my phone to find her picture

AMANI *takes out his phone, starts scrolling.*

Buried deep in my camera roll by now
But there, nonetheless
And usually I'm not one to get too excited but
DAMN!
–

*Maybe he shows an audience member a picture
of her.*

We'd look good together, innit?
–

I'd be lying if I said I wasn't
Low-key
Absolutely
Bricking it…
'Cause I've never done this sorta thing before…
Like,
Obviously I don't mean dating
'Cause all you gotta do is look at me to know
That I have NO PROBLEMS
In the 'getting gyal' department
If I do say so myself…
But yeah,
I've never done the 'blind dating' thing.
I can't lie
I always thought it was something that sad, old,
gyal-less people did when they were bored
And lonely…
But here I am:
Not sad
Not old
And definitely not gyal-less!
Might be a bit bored, though.
Might be why I agreed to it.
Might be why I thought 'yeah… why not?
Just this once.'

BRIANNA   I mean,
            I thought it was a dumb idea
            But I really wanted to put myself out there this
            summer.
            Say yes more.
            To everything.
            And I think I meant that more… creatively
            But I guess it can extend to… this stuff, too.

BOTH   'Cause how am I gonna have the summer to end
            all summers
            With no one to share it with?

            Beat.

AMANI   My friends set it up.

BRIANNA   Leema and KB…

AMANI   Leema yeah,
            She's like the second-best poet I know
            Second after me, of course.
            Can't lie,
            She's a bit too inna my love life
            But I've known her for time, innit.
            Since primary-school days.
            And we came up together, so I let it slide.

BRIANNA   And KB:
            He's this bad-boy music producer…
            The first person I met on the scene
            That wasn't a complete dickhead…
            He let me photograph some of his events when
            I was just starting out
            So I kinda owe it to him to say yes sometimes.
            And anyways,
            Him and Leema are kinda joined at the hip these
            days,
            So her ideas

AMANI   Become his ideas

BOTH   Becomes 'their idea'

BRIANNA   Becomes:
            (*Leema. A bit posh.*) 'So we had this idea…'

AMANI   (*KB. MLE accent, sounds permanently zooted.*)
               'And you're gonna wanna say no…'

BRIANNA   (*Leema.*) 'You're gonna think you're too cool
               for it
               Because you think you're too cool for
               everything…'

AMANI   (*KB.*) 'But there's this girl – '
               I said no.
               At first.
               And I was quick wid it.
               Armed wid it.
               Word already on the back of my tongue as soon as
               she said the word 'idea' –
               But then KB was like,
               (*KB.*) 'Listen,
               She's creative, like you
               She takes pictures
               And she's like…
               Your type to a T, bro.'
               And just as my mind started imagining all the
               possibilities –
               'Cause really and truly,
               I'm not that picky –
               As long as she's melanated –
               He pulls out his phone
               And pulls up her picture…

BRIANNA   (*Leema.*) 'He's cute, right?'
               Leema said,
               Handing me the phone.
               And she's not exactly… wrong.
               But also, like… if you think he's so cute, you
               date him!
               Hypothetically of course,
               'Cause the only men that girl has ever liked
               Have been fictional.
               –
               So yeah,
               I guess he's cute.
               He's got this

Boyish
Familiar
Thing about his face…
Shoulders all relaxed
Showing levels of laid-back that
I can only aspire to.
This
Look –
A smile –
In his eyes
Contagious
Like he's someone I could've known my whole
life…
–

So, yeah.
He's just okay.
I guess I could look at his face for a couple
of hours.
Yeah.
–

Leema airdrops the picture to me.
She says it's so I can look at it
Whenever I feel like changing my mind.

AMANI   (*KB.*) 'And don't take it too serious, Bri…
Amani's not that guy.
I know you, you'll say yes then find ten reasons
not to go.'
–

You know what I said before about not really
having a type like that…?
Yeah, well
I lied.
'Cause it's her.
'Cause in the pic,
She's laughing
All unguarded
Open-hearted
Something… different.

Beat.

Her name's 'Brianna'

BRIANNA   His name's 'Amani'

AMANI   She's 'of the islands'
Like moi.
So I'm thinking…
(*Demonstrating his waistline.*)
Carni
For the
Second date?

BRIANNA   He's Jamaican.
And don't get me wrong, I love my people dem
But…

She shudders jokily.

AMANI   She's a student.
A student artist.
And I don't know how those two things really fit
together
'Cause me, personally…
My type of art can't be taught, you get me?
It's why I didn't go uni.

BRIANNA   He doesn't go uni.
His first strike in my mum's eyes.
You know, I told her that only way I'd get a degree
Was if it was in photography.
She said that freelance is just a fancy word for
'broke-by-choice',
Said pictures don't pay rent,
'Dem nuh protect when tings guh left.'
But
My academic record was UNTOUCHABLE,
So she couldn't say no…
What she did say, though…
Was 'Just wait.'
'Cause the real world always wins,
Seeps from the corners of your perfect picture
To swallow you whole
Said one day it'll catch you slipping
And remind you where you actually are
So it's always important to hold onto control.

According to her, this summer was gonna show
me that truth.
So,
Yeah
I guess I've got a bit more than love stuff to prove.

Beat.

He's a writer.
A poet.
And that's somehow worse 'cause…

She shudders.

After God, fear men who are good with their
words.

AMANI   She's a photographer.
And I don't really mind
'Cause
Cameras love me
Naturally.
And maybe, if the date goes well… she'll get my
fit pics right.

BRIANNA   I remember this one time
I was at a networking thing with a friend when
this 'poet' tried to move to me using modified
Dave bars??

*AMANI becomes the 'poet' and drops the
aforementioned 'modified Dave bars'.*

I hope this one's got a bit more to say.

AMANI   Writing's always been my thing
Like,
When I was younger, I didn't really get it.
I'd just scribble stuff down.
Stuff I couldn't say out loud.
But after Mum…
I started writing letters to her.
Poems…
But I didn't know it, then.
About school

About Dad
About Nan
Fussing over me every second of the day
I'd...
Fold them up
Slide them into envelopes
Like I was gonna send them somewhere
Like heaven's got a post box,
Or something.

Beat.

But it helped.
Made me feel like there could be power in my
words
Like my words could cross dimensions
To her.
And it just stuck.
And now it's what I do
For anyone who'll listen.
Don't get me wrong, though
Back in the day...
Poetry... it weren't really the vibe
Like
The mandem love to act like they're my biggest
fans now, yeah
But back then
You couldn't be out here with a notebook and pen
talking about 'roses are red'
Expecting anything but laughter –
That's what Dad said would happen anyway –
So naturally,
I had to switch it up.
Bars are bars, though, innit?
Start spitting them like freestyles
And suddenly
It's a whole different story.
–
After that, I got bold.
Went from pen and page to the stage
Started pouring out my soul
And getting it handed back in clicks

And the performance –
The presentation –
Became a new kind of hit
And then suddenly
On stage
I weren't that scared and…
Lonely kid
And people GASSEDDDDDD IT.
So, yeah.
It all just fell into place.

–

I don't know many photographers
But I feel like
We're one and the same.
'Cause we're both capturing parts of the human
experience
Just in different ways.
/ I wonder how she'd capture me.

BRIANNA   / I wonder how he'd capture me.

Beat.

When I've finally picked my twist-out to
perfection
I send a mirror pic to my girls
Phone camera
Not a 'camera' camera.

–

They say a picture's worth a thousand words
But I still feel like I talk too much
And when I don't talk, I think too much
About all the stuff you're not supposed to think
about when you're on your way to meet
someone that you don't even know but feel like
you do
That might not even like you
For you.

Beat.

And maybe that's why I like pictures
Because they don't lie.

>   What you see is what you get.
>   There's no space in the frame for the mess in your
>   head
>   And I guess,
>   You can't… make a photo feel like it's not good
>   enough.
>   It just is.
>   And to be honest,
>   When I'm behind that camera
>   It's the only time that I'm really in charge
>   'Cause I know what the lens sees
>   But I can't control how he's gonna see me
>   So –

AMANI   We're meeting at six.

BRIANNA   On the dot.

AMANI   'Cause according to Leema,
          (*Leema.*) 'Brianna's got this thing about time.
          Just don't mess her about.'

BRIANNA   See,
          We're meeting at this
          Boujee-ass jazz and soul bar/lounge
          In the far SE

AMANI   Crystal Pally
          Live music and chill vibes
          Straight trip on the Windrush
          'But still can't pay back the victims of the
          Windrush Scandal'
          Line.

BRIANNA   Home of
          Low lighting
          Teefing drink prices
          The occasional open-mic and –

AMANI   That's it.
          That's all I'm allowed to know.
          (*KB.*) 'And that's all she knows, too, yeah?
          So trust me broooooo.'

BRIANNA   And I do,
Trust them.
But I don't know if I really trust myself
Not to… you know,
Completely mess this up.
And it's not like that's something I do often or
anything –
Mess things up,
But that kind of makes it even worse, you know?
No?

Beat.

(*Leema.*) 'And it's really no pressure,
'Cause I know how you can be…'
But I've spent so long asking for permission to
be me
I don't know if I've got the facilities…

BOTH   I shake off my nerves
Which are clinging to me
Like sweat
Making my skin feel all tight
Like I need to change out of it.

AMANI   And I put on one of my favourite tunes…
So I can feel like I'm in one of those 'getting
ready' movie montages.

BRIANNA   And not too much on the music choice, yeah.
'Cause

AMANI   It is
NEVER

BRIANNA   Too early

AMANI   Fi dancehall!

AMANI *gets dressed while* BRIANNA *does her
hair/make-up. They're not in the same time
or place, but as the music plays, it turns into this
kind-of duet.*

***

AMANI   I check my fit in the mirror
           Keeping an
           Eye out
           For marks
           Crushed corners
           Unflattering folds
           Scanning myself
           For imperfections…
           And I come to the conclusion –
           Yes.
           Me,
           Myself,
           And I,
           Unanimously agree,
           That I look GOOD!
           Whew!
           Yeah, she's gonna be picking her jaw up off the
           floor, 'cause WHAT?
           And I hate to be one of those fashion
           motherfuckers
           'Cause
           Red flag, I've been told…
           But I really put that shit on!
           'Cause these man think
           That they can just throw on a pair of baggy jeans
           And call it style…
           I've got the
           Baggy jeans AND baggy tee combo
           So how about that?!
           –

           I put on my Air Forces –
           Not my everyday ones,
           my WEDDING ONES!
           What?
           They're just THAT clean!
           And it all comes together…
           Perfection!
           I'm looking like…
           Like…
           The Fresh Prince of South!
           Like,

If people still used the word 'swag'
then that would be the word of the day
For this
MONSTER
Of a fit.
'Cause if you look good
Other people feel good.
And if other people feel good,
You don't even really gotta *be* good.
But right now
As I scrutinise
My reflection winking back at me
I think it's safe to say I'm good in BOTH ways!

BRIANNA   I manage to fix my hair into the
PERFECT
Fluffy
Twist-out
Surprisingly undisturbed by the little bonnet
mishap earlier,
And I won't lie, I was worried
'Cause I spent so long prepping last night
And I was scared it was gonna be one of them
ones where you're halfway through
unravelling the twists only to find that they're still
damp in the middle…
But all is well.
And now's about the time where I actually start
getting dressed,
But
I'm looking
Practically
Rummaging
Through my drawers
Looking for the clothes that I SWEAR I laid out
last night…
I'm thinking that maybe my mum moved them,
Tidied them up by mistake…
But I'm searching and searching
And they're actually nowhere to be found!
Like,

I've basically emptied out my whole wardrobe at
this point and they're dead GARN.
Thin air.
And I start just
kind of
fiddling with my hair
Because I've known about the Tube delays since
last night
And I was hoping to leave early to have
contingency time
And –
I scan my surroundings one more time 'cause
I don't wanna go blaming who
Realistically
I KNOW
Is to blame
But honestly, unless there's a dripped-out duppy
living in my room…
I know exactly where my stuff is!
–

I march out of my room to the top of the stairs and
before I can even scream,
I hear the sound of little footsteps running across
the hallway.
They must've sensed me.
'Nevaeh! Aliyah!'
–

They screech in reply, and I follow the footprints
in the carpet down the stairs and into the
living room.
Their hiding place is betrayed by the giggles
coming out from behind the curtains,
That and the
Stripy-socked feet sticking out from underneath.
My mum shouts from the kitchen,
That we should: 'Stop e noise!'
But really and truly
What needs to be done
Is for her to tell her kids to stop teefing my stuff!
I pull the curtain away to reveal the two
Guilty

Suspects.
Nevaeh's wearing my skirt, which is wayyy too
big for her likkle ten-year-old teefing self
And Aliyah,
Who's actually taller than me –
Something about those middle-child genes –
Is stretching out my top!

—

I go for Aliyah first, and she's resistant,
So naturally I opt to physically take the top for
myself!
It's easy enough… I think…
But she's squirming under my weight like crazy
And before I know it,
Nevaeh's…
Nah,
Is this child actually on my back?!
See how I get ganged up on in this house?
It's gotta be a conspiracy.

—

'You little b– '
We struggle some more,
And she's bigger than me so she's kind of got the
upper hand…
Using her
Limb length
To her advantage
So that all I can see are flying legs…
Nevaeh covers my eyes with her hands,
But she's like four-foot-nothing
So I throw her off with ease,
My hand clasped onto my contraband skirt
Which is halfway over her head at this point.
Aliyah takes this as an opportunity to escape from
under me,
and crawls out… almost victorious…
when I hear a
Riiiiiiiiiiiip.

—

Time stops.

My sisters freeze,
'cause they know it just got serious.
—

I look down at the piece of torn fabric in my hand
My eyes travelling to what used to be my top
around Aliyah's neck.
Hand.
Lap.
Hand.
Lap.
'Fucking.
Adopted.
RATS.'

Beat.

Just saying, but if they go missing…
It wasn't me.

AMANI   The only thing that's missing
Is the trim.
Not just… any trim
But THEE trim
The trim that's gonna turn everything up
By like,
One hundred.
The trim that's gonna have her
Tripping
stumbling
Falling
In love
At first…
Vibe.

Beat.

And you may ask,
'Amani, why have you left such an important
Monumental
Life-altering
Trim
For the day of?'
But you see,

This trim needs to be crispy
Crispy like Walkers,
Crispy like how I like the edges of my fried
plantain
(*Makes a CRUNCH sound.*)
Like,
My hair isn't even too overgrown, right now
But that line-up haffi be sharp!
Sharp like a machete
Sharp like my auntie's tongue
So sharp that you could slice your finger on it!

He pretends to cut his finger on his hairline.

That sharp!
—

And she's worth it, like
I swear, that pic made me sit up a little straighter
That smile, yeah, it put me on my best
behaviour…
And it's not like I've got anything to prove –
'Cause I don't –
But if this was a nineties R'n'B music video she'd
have man doing BACKFLIPS to get her attention,
D'you get it?
So I've gotta come correct.
—

I've got a slot around lunchtime
Which is kinda
Sorta
A bit too
Soon
Because it means that my date's getting closer
Which means the pressure's getting WORSER
Which means my armpit's getting sweatier and –

AMANI *sniffs his armpit.*

Yeah.

BRIANNA   I narrowly avoid a crisis by having a back-up fit
           But I'd be lying if I said
           It didn't bother me

That my sisters have already managed to upset my
day…
That the first thing I've tried to do today…
Didn't go to plan.
'Cause anyone who knows me,
Knows I'm a planner.
That I like things to be perfect
To a T,
My friends call it being a bit uptight,
My cousin who studies psychology calls it
'undiagnosed neurodivergence',
I just call it… the path of least anxiety??
Like,
I thought stress-free was the goal?
So what if I have to control every aspect of my
day to achieve it…
See,
The old Brianna would've cancelled the whole
thing already,
Right after my bonnet decided to go
Walkabout in the night.
But the *new* Brianna –
You're looking at her –
Has put on a new, un-torn, fit that she loves…
That she hopes he'll like, too.

***

AMANI   I'm about to leave
Ready to have
Blessings
Bestowed
Upon my head-top
When my phone starts ringing.
I'm half expecting it to be Leema or KB
Checking to see I haven't backed out or
anything…
Or maybe my dad
Reminding me to take the chicken out the freezer –
Note to self:
Take the chicken out the freezer –
But it's my nan.

Nana Eileen but we call her Phillis
Because
Well
Mi nuh know
And it's just like,
Why is my nan calling me at twelve p.m. on
a Saturday?
Something must be wrong.
So I answer.
—

'Hi Nan,
Everything good?'
(*Phillis. Fading Jamaican accent.*) 'No.'
And then she does that really long pause that old
people do
That low-key worrying pause…
And my heart starts doing a thing I've only felt
once before –
And my mind starts knocking on thoughts with
boarded-up doors –
And I'm already springing into action
Ready to sprint
To her yard –
(*Phillis.*) 'Mi need – '
'What do you need, Nan?'
(*Phillis.*) 'Help. Please.'
And then the phone line goes dead.
And I'm thinking…
I'm thinking…
Has someone kidnapped my nan?
Is someone holding my nan hostage in her house?
Was that the proof-of-life call??
Fuck.
I run out
Kinda tiptoe out
Because…
Air Forces –
What?
My nan would understand.
And as I'm shutting the door,
I think of the haircut slot

That I called in advance to reserve…
Trim or Grandma
Grandma or trim…
–
Grandma.
Obviously??
Who do you lot think I am??
My barber's got my back anyways.

BRIANNA   I'm about to leave,
Ready to take on
Whatever the day throws at me…
Okay, I lied –
Maybe not
'Whatever'
I'm not quite there… YET!
But ready to start the journey, at least!
And when I say,
'about to leave'
I mean,
Door open
One foot over the frame
Wind already catching my face,
'about to leave'
But just as the rest of my body attempts to follow…
I hear my mum call from somewhere in the house,
(*Mum. South London accent, but code-switches
into patois.*) 'Brianna, you garn? I need you
downstairs!'
And I stop for a second,
'Cause I REALLY need to consider my options
here.
If I don't answer…
Pretend I've already gone,
And just close the door REALLY quietly…
Maybe I can escape without being pulled into
whatever it is she's calling me for!
But if I don't…
I'll be a bad daughter.
And personally, I don't know if I can handle that.
Yeah,

The eldest daughter syndrome in this one is
STRONG,
I'm working on it.
Turns out I'm working on a lot of things.
–

She calls out again,
And her voice has got a bit of bass in it this time.
The kind of bass that feeds the growing lump in
my throat…
I fold in without thinking –
Like laundry –
Shoulders first,
Then mouth,
And I pull myself back through the door.
I'm even hungry, too,
And I could probably do with the extra time to
grab some munch
But –
(*Mum.*) 'Brianna?'
Responsibilities or food
Food or responsibilities…
You already know which one I'm choosing.

***

AMANI   I get to my nan's
            It's a 53 and a 47
            Away…
            In the wrong direction
            But I'm firming it.
            I tried calling her two more times on her
            housephone on the way
            And it just rung out
            Which made me rush even more.
            I bang on the door
            Frantic
            Ready to beat
            Down
            whoever's got my nan
            and I wait.
            –

            –

Soon enough,
I hear footsteps
And the
Click
Clack
Click
Of a door being taken off the latch…
–

(*Phillis*.) 'Amani! Why yuh bang pon di door,
suh? Mi can still hear good, enuh!'
And I'm just
Kind of floored
Because here I am
Expecting some
Big
Hench
Proper
'Kidnapper'
Looking someone
To open the door…
But instead,
It's my
Much
tinier
Grandma.
Looking at me like
I'm mad.
'Nan, you're okay?'
(*Phillis*.) 'It nuh mi did call yuh?'
'Well yeah, but you said you needed help?
I thought you were in trouble.'
(*Phillis*.) 'Mi need help, yes.
With di TV!'
What?
–

I follow her inside
Chest
Rising
And
Falling
As the adrenaline

Built up on the bus
Escapes my body.
I'm kinda quiet at this point
'Cause I don't want her to know I was
panicking…
But it doesn't help that the house is hot with steam
from the kitchen…
–

I get to the living room
The living room with that
Grandma's
Living room smell –
If you know you know –
Eyes doing a quick scan of the national anthem
scroll on the wall
Because Jamaica land we love, for real!
And sure enough
The TV…
is looking a bit off, still.
(*Phillis*.) 'Amani, see how di ting mashup suh?
One minute, *Emmerdale* there, next minute…
garn!'
'Nan!'
'Amani!'
'Nan, it's not broken.
The HDMI cable's been knocked out, that's all.'
(*Phillis*.) 'Hmmm mi nah bada with dem tings deh
suh. Technology an computers.'
She turns towards the door to the kitchen.
'I know, Nan.
But remember last time this happened and
I showed you exactly where to plug it in?'
(*Phillis*.) 'Hmmm.'
Yeah,
She's checked out.
–

–

I work my magic in the living room
While Nan works her magic in the kitchen
And yeah
All I have to do is plug in a cable…

Light work…
But to her,
I'm an engineer!
'Cause the back of the TV?
Alla dat wire an cable an plug?
Is NONE of her business, for real.
—

I shout that I'm done through the kitchen door.
That her programme's back on –
Some new joint.
Bingo
Meets
Deal or No Deal
Meets
Catchphrase
And I don't know.
Can I be annoyed?
'Cause I really thought it was serious,
Miss-my-slot-at-the-barber's serious
Risk-my-monumental-trim serious
And I'm like the
Third grandchild
That she could've called??
—

It's good to see her,
Though.
Good to see the house.
Good to smell the house.
Good to eat the –
I really don't come here enough.

Beat.

She calls me from the kitchen,
(*Phillis.*) 'Amani! Yuh fadda feed yuh?'
'No ma'am!'
(*Phillis.*) (*Kisses teeth.*) 'Come.'
—

I practically leap
Jump
Hop
Skip

into the kitchen.
The hot air hits me first
Then the smell
That's been
Filling up
The house
And my nose
Making my mouth water like
river
Lake
Ocean.
And I know I shouldn't…
Like,
I really shouldn't
Like,
I'm late as it is
Like,
I actually have things to do today
Like –
Like I'm actually kind of hungry
Now that I think about it

–

Like,
What kind of grandson would I be if I didn't take
the food?

Beat.

Nan's always there, yeah
A bit extra sometimes but
She's the sun that my family revolves around
And without her gravitational pull
I know we'd crash into darkness.

–

I make my way to the chair
Fried dumpling and ackee 'n' saltfish
already making its way
Down my oesophagus…
And it's a shirt-off kind of occasion
'Cause I don't wanna mark up the tee
But of course, I'll need a mini-shower to shed that
fish smell…

I'll be quick.
In and out.
Trust.
–

–

–

I wake up
And it's almost two.
Thirty.
Fuck.
Someone needs to do a study on this food, you
know!
'Cause it's not normal
How it's just MADE for the soul.
How it just made my sense of time go like that!
–

I hug Nan goodbye
Say thank you
For the food
Halfway through my last mouthful.
She says thank you
For fixing the TV.
Halfway through the hug,
And she pushes a twenty-pound note into my hand
like we just did a drug deal
Hollywood-style
(*Phillis*.) 'Shhhhh. Don't tell yuh fadda, yeah?'
Now THIS is why I love coming here!
Dad tries
And I love him for it
But he's all rules and responsibility
Said I shouldn't get anything I didn't earn
But he's spent decades earning less than what he
deserves so
Respectfully
I'mma just do me
Guilt-free, you know?

Beat.

I say thank you again
I say I gotta run.

And indeed
I dip.

***

BRIANNA   I should've dipped when I had the chance.
I make my way down the stairs,
Slowly,
Anticipating.
I still haven't even let her know I'm still in the
house
'Cause of that one time she told me that saying,
'Yes, Mummy?' was answering back…
Yeah –
I'm not sure, either.
'You called me, Mummy?'
She looks me up and down,
(*Mum.*) 'Hmmm. Why you dress up suh?'
'I'm going out with friends. I told you last week.'
(*Mum.*) 'Hmmm okay. I need you to take the
washing out.'
'Can't Aliyah do it, Mum?'
But then Aliyah pokes a smug face around the
corner and goes:
(*Aliyah.*) 'Liar! I heard her on the phone saying
she's going to meet – '
I scramble,
'I guess I'll take the washing out.'
And Aliyah's head disappears like a Whack-A-Mole.
(*Mum.*) 'Hmmm. And when you're done with that,
I need you to sweep the upstairs hallway.'
'But I really need to g–'
(*Mum.*) 'I don't know who taught you this attitude
you know, must be them white children
at university.'
'But Mummy – '
(*Mum.*) 'But what? Guh do de tings dem.'
–

It's annoying
'Cause it's exactly what I thought –
What I knew –
Was gonna happen

But I don't know,
Maybe I was hoping for a little bit of grace today?
Especially since I KNOW that my two equally-as-
capable siblings are upstairs doing
Rass!
–

'Okay Mummy.'
I make my way to the washing machine and
unload it
New fit,
And I'm gonna sweat it out before I've even made
it out the house…
What a tragedy.
While I'm hanging out the clothes in the garden,
I see Nevaeh sticking her tongue out at me from
the upstairs window
And I make the
Ugliest
Most
Nightmare-inducing
Face back
'Cause who is she actually looking at?
Demon.
And I mourn the freedom I could've had if I had
just run out when I had the chance!
Once I'm done,
I get to sweeping,
And I think about how this must've been what
Cinderella felt like.
Cinderella starring Brandy –
Obviously.
And I find myself wishing for a saving grace,
A fairy godmother,
That will get me out of my chores,
To the open mic –
I mean, ball
So that I can finally meet –
You thought I was gonna call him a prince,
didn't you
NEVER that.
So I can finally meet the random guy that my
friends insist I'll like so much.

I finish sweeping,
And make my way back to the kitchen where my
mother dearest is waiting,
broom in hand.
'I've finished.'
She looks me up and down again.
(*Mum.*) 'I need you to sweep down here as well.'
Nah, you've gotta be kidding me!
Sorry,
Did you forget about the other kids you have or
what?
—

Is what I say in my head.
—

But I value my life,
So instead I say,
'Okay.'
—

(*Mum.*) 'And leave time after for the dishes.'
'But we literally have a dishwasher?'
Oop.
She gives me a look.
That 'don't try me'
Universal
Black mum look
That brings you right back
To when you were ten.
Time travel in an expression.
And I shut my mouth real quick.
She nods, satisfied,
And I muster up some courage,
Something I've been tryna do more this summer,
And say,
'Mummy, I really don't wanna be late to see my
friends. If I sweep upstairs, could Aliyah
maybe take the dishes this one time?'
(*Mum.*) 'Aliyah's got street dance today. Chores
first, then go.'
I look at the time and sigh,
Start that
Kind of
Tapping

On my thigh
'Cause I really do have things to do
And she's already teefed a whole hour –
'Look. Mummy. My train's coming soon and if
I stay I won't have time for food – '
That look again.
–

It's okay.
It's all good.
Chores first, then go.

***

AMANI   I get to the barber's
Just before three –
Shit –
And the thing about this barber's, yeah
Is that it's the same one,
Just off Queens Road,
That I've been coming to since I was four.
See, Mum liked it long
Braidable
But when she passed –
Even though I was big fourteen –
Dad decided he didn't want me looking like 'him
darta' no more…
But yeah.
I've been
Tethered to this place
Ever since.

Beat.

I open the door and it
Chimes
That
Familiar
Chime.
Reggae
Plays
Low
Like background music
To your thoughts.

The low hum of conversation
Seasons the air –
All-purpose –
And
Heads snap towards me
Like predators
To prey…
But then
their eyes soften
When they realise that it's just
(*Leroy. South London accent, but code-switches
into patois.*) 'Likkle Mani!'
Says Leroy,
The owner.
Arms outstretched
Towel in one hand, phone in the other.
And his forehead's creased with stress
Or concentration
Or the unmistakable markings of a durag
tied wayyy too tight.
'Wagwan, Uncs. Busy shop today?'
I say –
Kind of shout –
Because I'm in a losing battle with the buzz of
clippers and the choir of voices
In symphony across the packed space.
Leroy waves a hand
Dismissive,
'Cause he obviously didn't hear me
And I step over some Clarks to get to him
Scanning the space
Noting every chair, already filled –
Weird –
And looking for mine.
'Uncle Wayne around? I scheduled a cut with him
earlier.'
–
He's not really my uncle.
Not by blood.
But he's known my dad longer than I've been born
And I wouldn't dream

Nightmare
Of anyone else touching my head!
–

Leroy kinda stares at me
Nah, through me
Blinks like
I'm speaking some next language
Like I'm just another customer lining up
In his uncharacteristically crowded shop…
But then he says
(*Leroy*.) 'Ummm. Yuh jus miss him.'
'What do you mean, just?'
(*Leroy*.) 'Him leff… about an hour ago… Yeah.
Him garn.'
And he's rubbing the back of his neck as he says it,
Head hung like he just told me someone died
And internally,
I'm like
Nah.
Nah nah nah.
'Cause that just can't be right, can it?
'What do you mean, garn? Like to the shops or – '
(*Leroy*.) 'Nah. Airport. Back to yard.'
What?
'What?!'
What???!!!
And he must sense my
Literal
Organs
Shutting
Down
In panic
Because then he says,
(*Leroy*.) 'You know I've got you, young G.'
'Ah, you've got me? So you're gonna magic
Wayne right back here to cut my hair, yeah?'
He laughs and taps my shoulder in response.
(*Leroy*.) 'Ay Junior! Sort out Likkle Mani fi mi,
please!'
–

I turn around slowly
'Cause I don't know no 'Junior'

And I'm met with the… kind-of-smiling,
kind-of-not,
Face of a man
that's giving off some very
Odd
Strange
Peculiar
Vibes.
Like
I don't know if he wants to eat me…
Or if that's just how his face is set up.
—

(*Leroy*.) 'Wayne nephew dat. He's new.'
And I feel a
Visceral
Pang
Because I can't be putting my whole future into
the hands of no one that's 'new'!
And as if on cue
The clippers Junior was fumbling with clatter to
the ground.
'No.'
I say without thinking
(*Leroy*.) 'We yuh mean, no? Wha'appen to yuh?'
Straight patwa so you know he's serious
And I try open my mouth again
But the look he gives me makes me forget that I'm
the taller one.

I take a deep breath
Eyes darting
From Leroy
To Junior
To the mirror
And along the jagged line of my front taper.

Beat.

It's now or never.
'You've got me, yeah? I'm ready.'
And before I can ever register my choice
He's ushering me over to the chair
In the

Far
Left
Corner.
Like some criminal!
The regret comes faster than the realisation…
But I can't go meet gyal trimless, can I?

Beat.

I hear some unreserved
chuckling in the background
And I say a little prayer as I
Slide myself
Back into the seat.
Junior puts the cape over me.
Big hands fastening it behind my neck
All clumsy
With all the delicacy
And finesse
Of
Godzilla
And I gulp.
'I just want a little off the top, yeah? Even out my
fade. And line me up good, please Boss!'
He doesn't reply
But picks up the razor anyway
All slow
Suspicious
like he's about to go all Sweeney Todd on me
I pray harder
Even though I'm not even religious like that.

BRIANNA   I finally escape
My
Personal
Cinderella
Story:
Eldest daughter edition,
and allow myself to revel in the warm light of the
sun on my skin.
I'm finally free
And if I said I was hungry before,

I am STARVING now.
'Cause I skipped breakfast, innit,
And I thought I'd be able to last…
But my own mother
Just doesn't wanna see me thrive.
—

There's only one place I really need to be right
now…
One
Specific
Place
That I'm craving:
Annie's!
Cute little West Indian West African fusion set-up
in the innermost corner of Brixton Market, a ten-
minute walk away from yard,
Home to some of the best
Most
Flakiest
Most
Flavourful
Patties ever tasted,
Second after my grandma's, of course.
And even though gentrification's got them hiking
up their prices like it wouldn't cost like
a pound back a yard,
I'm still faithful!
—

'A chicken patty, please, Auntie.'
She blinks at me.
(*Auntie Annie. Thick patois.*) 'We nuh have dat.'
Okay.
'Beef?'
(*Auntie Annie.*) 'It run out.'
'Saltfish?'
(*Auntie Annie.*) 'It run out.'
'Well whatever's there then.'
Auntie practically cuts her eye after me as she
slides the patty into a paper bag
Which makes me even more excited,
'Cause the ruder the servers are,

The better the food tastes.
What?
Them's the rules!
I pay and almost skip out of the shop,
Mouth watering long before I even had it in my
hands…
'Cause like,
Someone needs to do a study on this food,
you know!
'Cause it's not normal
How it's just MADE for the soul.
How it's just made me forget about the madness of
earlier like that!
—

I take a bite before I'm even through the door,
And I'm so distracted by the
Explosion
Of goodness
In my mouth…
That I don't notice the little boys with water guns
on the street front…
Stopping
And aiming…
Right at me,
My pattie,
And my
Perfect
Fluffy
Twist-out.

AMANI   See,
It doesn't start too bad.
Like
I can see in the mirror
And he's blessing the ting, still…
It's only when I start seeing
Previously undiscovered planes of forehead
Start to show
That my forming smile
Drops.
—

'Hey, Boss!'
He ignores me.
'Boss! Can we stop for a minute? I think you're
pushing me back.'
He doesn't stop.
Fuck.
He won't stop.
I can just see my forehead surface area increasing
In pace with my quickening heartbeat…

BRIANNA   I feel the cold of the water first,
Icy and sharp…
Concentrated.
Right in the middle of my face.
And then I feel the invasion of wetness
As my clothes start
Clinging
And the paper bag holding my patty starts
Disintegrating
And my hair starts

–

Shrinking.

AMANI   I shoot a desperate look to Leroy,
Wondering how I even found myself in
Junior's chair.
Look back in the mirror,
And I swear I can see this man smirking –

–

But then
The unthinkable
The unimaginable
The inconceivable happens..
And my man sneezes.

–

And it's not no
Cute little –
Tiny little –
Baby sneeze
No.
It's a loud-ass –
Grown-man –

Hard-back –
Razor-still-connected –
Chunk-out-of-my-hairline sneeze!
–

–

Oh my god.
Chunk
Out
Of
My
Hair
Line.
Junior finally speaks,
And he just says,
(*Junior*.) 'Bomboclarttttttttt.'
–

–

–

I black out.

BRIANNA   It all happens so fast.
I drop the patty.
The gentrification-priced patty
That I've been craving from morning
And my hands fly up to my hair,
Which is becoming increasingly dense with water
Contracting
More
And
More
With every
Hyperventilated
Breath…
The kids run off before I can even register their
crime,
'Cause this has gotta be a crime, right?
A hate crime, even.
'Cause how are you gonna ruin what might have
been the best twist-out ever achieved on
natural hair?
How are you gonna ruin a WEEK of careful

Strategic
planning
To make sure I could be at maximum curl capacity
Maximum ME capacity
Today?
Like,
Those curls weren't even giving high definition…
They were giving 4K…
Like, I thought the bonnet mishap from earlier was
a lucky save but…
Now?
That –
That lump in my throat…
The one I mentioned earlier,
Begins to make its presence
Ever known.
Because now, more than anything –
And don't hate me –
I just wanna go home.

AMANI   When I come back into my body,
I can see
That he's tried to fix it.
I lean forward in the mirror
And notice
That it no longer looks like
Someone took a bite
Out of my trim…
No.
'Cause now
It's just a straight up diagonal line!

Beat.

I –
I think I'm gonna cry.

–

I think I'm gonna pass out.

–

No word of a lie
I think I'm gonna crash out

–

The pain hits my stomach first
Then my chest
Then it's all over.
Searing
Hot
Red.
–

Is this what dying feels like?

BRIANNA   I turn around,
'Cause I'm still in the shop,
And the same Auntie who cut her eye at me just
moments earlier…
Shoots a look at me
And in that moment,
I swear, she looks just like my mum.
Saying, 'this is what happens when you ramp
with me'.

Beat.

She registers my face as she registers my clothes,
drenched…
My hair, ruined…

AMANI   Leroy comes over to see why his favourite
customer's starting to hyperventilate.
He registers my face as he registers my injury.
And
All he says is,

BRIANNA   All she says is,

BOTH   'Hush.'

AMANI   Which is basically
Jamaican for

BRIANNA   'You're absolutely –

AMANI   Categorically –

BOTH   FUCKED'

AMANI   I snap back into reality
To find

Myself
Still
In this bloodclart chair!
I take one last look at Junior,
And I briefly consider asking him to just shave me
completely bald.
'Cause anything
Would be better than this.

BRIANNA   'This isn't real life.'

AMANI   I kind of splutter.
'Cause actually
Nah.
And then I
Kind of
Start laughing –

BRIANNA   Crying –

AMANI   Laughing more.
Because what the actual fuck is my life right now?

BRIANNA   Like… I feel like I've done everything right till
now

AMANI   So why's
My hairline
A crooked line right now?

BRIANNA   Right on the edge of fight or flight right now?

AMANI   I'm
Looking in the mirror
Tryna to find a semblance of the self I came in with
A pumped-up ego bracing for my monumental
trim and
Thinking of the girl that I almost had a chance
with…
Thinking of the world
That was placed on my image
And how it's all come down.
And how it's feeling like when Dad first buzzed
off what Mum called my crown

And then suddenly I'm on a stage
But my words fail me now.

Beat.

Leroy tries to catch me on my way out, card
reader in hand
But I float past him
Like a ghost.
—

He doesn't even bother shouting after me to pay.
I think he feels bad
'Cause he's the one that sent me to my death.

***

BRIANNA   I run out of Annie's
Before I start bawling.

BOTH   The air hits me like bricks.

BRIANNA   I keep an eye out for my shooters, but I'm shaking.
Maybe from the cold of the water
But also from the anxiety that's been threatening
to boil over since my sisters stole my clothes.
—

I stop for a minute.
And blink back some

AMANI   Big man
Badman
Tears

BOTH   And when I've calmed down enough,
I pull my phone out
And call the GC.

AMANI   Soon enough,
The faces of
Three of my boys:
Kaylen, Olu, and Adam
Appear on screen.
Adam says,
(*Adam.*) 'Yo, why you hiding? Come onto the
screen!'
(*Kaylen.*) 'Yeah, wagwan?'

I take a deep breath.
'I just left the barber's, innit.'
Olu starts peering into his camera suspiciously,
(*Olu.*) 'Oh yeahhhh. You're seeing that girl, innit?'
(*Kaylen.*) 'Ah what's her name? Something with
a B? – '
'It's Brianna.'
(*Adam.*) 'Yeahhh Brianna! My mate went college
with her, still!'
(*Kaylen.*) 'But weren't you just talking to – '
(*Olu.*) 'Shush, he's "reformed" now, remember?
Brianna's different, that's what you said, innit?'
(*Kaylen.*) 'Sorryyyyyy, didn't know you were in
love, big man.'
I sigh.
'Cause this is gonna be a looooong one
I can tell.
(*Adam.*) 'Show us the damage, then!'
Here goes…
'Mandem… it's bad.'
They echo with 'how bad?'
And I feel another tear prick the corner of my eye
That can go RIGHT back to where it came from!
Blink it back
Before they catch it.
'Just… don't do too much… 'cause I know you're
gonna –'
(*Kaylen.*) 'Come. On. To. The. Screen. Bro.'

–

Fuck it
I tentatively inch into the frame
Already regretting it.
I hear their reactions before I see them.
(*All of them.*) 'OOOOOOOOOHHHHHHH'
(*Adam.*) 'FUCK that's bad!'
(*Olu.*) 'Aye Amani, why's it lopsided?'
(*Kaylen.*) 'Aye Amani, why can I find the X and Y
value of that line?'
(*Adam.*) 'Aye Amani, why've you got a four-head
on one side… and a five-head on the other?'
'Not too much on me, guys. Please.'

Then Adam goes,
(*Adam*.) 'Can't lie… date's done. Plenty more fish
in your DMs, though, amirite?'
Which makes me physically
Recoil –
Though I don't show it.
(*Olu*.) 'In loving memory of: Amani's hairline.'
(*Kaylen*.) 'Gone but never forgotten.'
They break out into a fit of laughter
And I start seeing myself
On one of those
Funeral
Programmes
Badly photoshopped into some clouds…

BRIANNA   It takes me a minute before I can respond to all of
the concerned questions.
'I –
Um
Hey, I –
UGHHH.'
(*Esther*.) 'What's going on, Bri?'
Says Esther,
Her face big on the screen,
One eyebrow crooked up with worry…
Then Jessica goes,
(*Jessica. Northern*.) 'Yeah, what happened?
You're like… soaked!'
I take a deep breath
'I haven't been out long… I just left Annie's,
innit.'
(*Jessica*.) 'OMG I LOVE Annie's! I miss it loads
now I'm back home!'
But then Esther goes,
(*Esther*.) 'Okay but Annie's ain't a swimming
pool, is it? So are you gonna explain why
you're so wet?'
So I explain –
Breaths interrupting –
How I got ambushed by two little kids wielding
Two weapons of mass destruction…

And I kind of recount my day up until this point
And how it's gone
Less than to plan
So far…
(*Esther.*) 'Oh yeah, you're meeting that guy.
Amani?'
'Yeah. Well, I'm meant to be.'
Jessica laughs,
(*Esther.*) 'He was cute, as well. Still mad that you
don't know anything about him.'
(*Jessica.*) 'You… going on a "blind date"… never
thought I'd actually see the day, didn't even know
people still did that.'
(*Esther.*) 'Well it's part of her rebrand… this new,
"say yes to everything" Bri…'
And they must notice my face
'Cause they snap right back into caring mode,
'I don't know… I'm like… soaking wet.
My hair's messed up like…
If you'd seen me this morning I –
It's just not working out.'

AMANI   (*Olu.*) 'Okay but… on a serious note, whoever did
that to you must want you dead!'
'Okay okay I get it.
It's shit.
So what do I do?
'Cause I can't let her see me like this, man!'
There's a moment of silence
Before Kaylen speaks up,
(*Kaylen.*) 'I think a durag's gonna be your best
bet, bro.'
'A durag? She's gonna think I'm hiding a bad trim
from her!'
(*Kaylen.*) 'Okay but you are, though.'

Beat.

Then Olu offers,
(*Olu.*) 'Or consider this… he just goes anyway?
Just as he is? She might find it… (*Putting on
a 'girl' voice.*) endearing'

–
And even though he's joking,
That sticks with me.
–

(*Olu.*) 'Alright, alright, fine. Where's the nearest
Black hair shop? Where are you, Peckham?
High street's gonna be a goldmine.
Go there and cop one – '
(*Kaylen.*) 'Before literally anyone
Can see you… 'cause WHEW!
You are NOT in a position to be seen!'

BRIANNA   (*Jessica.*) 'Aww I wish I could hug you through
the screen, babe.'
I smile at that.
(*Esther.*) 'You're good, though, yeah? You been
doing those grounding exercise things?'
'Yeah, course. Always.'
(*Esther.*) 'And you've done your breathing?'
'Trying.'
(*Jessica.*) 'Good, 'cause it's all gonna be fine! Can
you go back home to change?'
'Nah, I don't think there's time. Plus, it's one of
dem ones where if I go back home, there'll be
a million chores waiting for me.'
(*Esther.*) 'That's okay. It looks bare sunny where
you are, you'll dry in no time!'
(*Jessica.*) 'AND your hair still looks good!'
'You think so?'
They both nod enthusiastically
(*Esther.*) 'And if you still hate it by the time you
calm down, you've got that emergency hairband
on your wrist for a reason.'
My chest begins to feel a little lighter.
And the new Brianna reminds me:
I'm a fighter
'Cause if this is what's on the other side…
I think I can keep going
After all.
They suggest walking it off,
And remind me of my still-empty stomach

Saying I should grab a festival for the road and
Hop on the
415
to SE,
Find a likkle park
Ask if I've got my camera with me,
Which I always do.
Headphones with me?
Wouldn't have left the house without them.
And just before I end the call,
Jessica adds,
(*Jessica.*) 'Don't forget to tell us how it goes!'

***

AMANI   The nearest Black hair shop isn't far
but with the backup of traffic from New Cross
sides,
The bus app won't even refresh
And I'm
very much
Definitely
Running out of time
But I manage to grab a durag
In 2000s-rapper-white
For cheap.
—

I try use the reflection of the shop window
To tie it –
Not unsuccessfully!
Show owner
Eyeing me.
And when I'm done,
I take myself in.
A new man.
Reborn.
And I don't know if it's just me…
But I think it kind of…
Elevates the fit, nah?
Like it was pretty up there already, come on now!
But the durag just adds…
A certain

How you say…
'Je ne sais quoi'?!

Beat.

Hmmm.
That's what we're going with.

BRIANNA   I don't know where I'm going,
'Cause I'm
What some may call
Directionally challenged
Especially when it comes to Southwark sides –
Google Maps has got my back
And it brings me in the direction of a nice, big
park that I don't think I've been to before.
I start following the path
And pull my camera out,
Which up until now
Has been in my bag behind,
Thankfully untouched by the little water situation
earlier.
–

I pull it out for a test, and it stops time.
Like, even when everything's moving too fast, or
too loud, or too messy… you press a button, and
it's still.
Frozen.
Just for a moment.
Like, no one's arguing, no one's rushing, no one's
stealing your clothes or dumping more on
your plate.
It's just…

She exhales.

AMANI   On the way back,
I wonder what I'm even gonna say to her
When we meet.
How I'm gonna say it…
'Cause you gotta
Plan
These things

And perfect them.
First impressions can really
Make or break
Shit,
And I'm tryna
Make it count.

–

Hmmm maybe:
'Yo, I swear I've seen you somewhere before!
Oh yeah… that's right, it was in my dreams.
The name's Amani.'
Nah.
Or:
'Yo, the streets call me Amani, but you can call
me yours.'
Ew. Who am I??
Okay okay
What about…
And bear with me, here…
But what about:
'Hey, I'm Amani.'

While AMANI *ponders his pick-up line,*
BRIANNA *snaps a picture in the park that could*
almost be of AMANI, *standing there.*

BOTH   Yeah.
              That's the one.

BRIANNA   Headphones on so
              I can feel a bit more
              I don't know…
              Grounded.
              Some R'n'B plays and I'm no longer surrounded
              And love is real again
              Check that pic on my phone
              And he's suddenly looking really leng
              And
              Yeah.
              This is why you don't listen to love songs before
              dates
              Don't wanna encourage the delusion.

–

I tell myself that by the time I'm back,
I'll basically be completely dry
And ready to take on the day,
For real this time.
'Cause London doesn't always love you back,
But sometimes she'll send her sun in apology.

***

AMANI   I'm standing at the bus stop,
Minding my business
When I see two guys
That look a bit older than me
Come round the corner across the road.
Straight away
There's this feeling right in the pit of my
stomach…
That the universe hasn't stopped fucking with me
just yet…
And I do that
Instinctive
Pre-G check-check
Check my posture, square my shoulders
Self-assured, but not a threat
Eyeing all my exits,
Steady rising breaths…
(*Guy 1.*) 'Yo! Swear that's my man that threatened
Squares last week!'
And somehow
I know they mean me
'Cause
Standing alone at the bus stop
I stick out like a sore thumb.
But I don't know them.
And I definitely don't know no 'Squares'
Fuck kinda name is that anyway?
Like, if I was a roadman, I'd wanna be named
suttin' like 'Dagger' or 'the 'A' man' or –
(*Guy 2.*) 'Yeah! He was wearing that same durag!
I remember it, a white one!'
And it's just like

Actually fuck my life!
I swear it was the only colour they had in the shop,
man…
'I don't know you!'
I shout
And I'm telling the truth
'I'm not who you think I am!'
And what else do you even say?
'I'm Amani. Just Amani!'
But that's the thing…
It don't really matter what I say 'cause
As much as I try to curate how I appear
Sometimes there ain't really no choice there.

Beat.

I wish I knew what to do with that.
This might be the kind of thing you'd ask your dad
If he really *saw* you like that

Beat.

Plus,
Mum tried when she was alive
Said to find power in what I *could* control
But,
She's gone so…
—
As they start to cross the road
I do
What is possibly
The worst thing
I could possibly do…
And I PACE IT.
It was fight or flight
And I chose FLIGHT
But
Obviously
That looks mad incriminating
To certain man…
(*Guy 2.*) 'Nah, that's defo him, you know!'
(*Guy 1.*) 'Yeah, why's he running?'

And even now
I'm barely even registering what's happening.
My feet are just moving
Carrying me away
As far as they can take me
Away from the bus stop.
I'm running…
But they're running, too
And there's two of them
So
Basically
I'm gonna die.
For the SECOND time today.
And I don't even know where I'm running to
But my brain's telling my legs
Faster
Quicker
Faster
Go
And they obey.
For now.
They're shouting after me now
(*Guy 1.*) 'Oi, durag!'
But can't lie,
I'm not even hearing what they're saying
'Cause I'm too busy bolting for my life.
And don't get me wrong,
I'm doing well.
Like,
I'm fast.
Like,
I was actually the fastest boy in year seven!
So
Maybe I'll make it to my date in one piece after all!
–
They're
So
Close
That
Their
Footsteps

Are
In
Sync
With
My
Heart
Beat
And just as my legs start getting tired
As my will to live starts to dissipate and
I think they're finally gonna get me
Gonna catch up
That they're gonna pounce
Or
Whatever it is
Mad people do…
I feel the spirit of Usain Bolt enter my body.
I feel a renewal as my legs take on a new energy
And I'm thinking that
To outsiders,
They must be going so fast that it looks like my
torso's just riding along on a cloud of dust
and smoke
All blurry and shit
Like Roadrunner!
I start turning corners
Fading
Faking
Running into backstreets
Jumping bollards
Fences
And park hedges…
Feel like I'm the main character in a low-budget
action movie!
And when I finally hear them cuss in defeat…
I start to smile
And then I laugh…
'Cause this is the second time the universe has
tried to off me today!
'Cause this is how boys that look like me go
missing
And I've got out by the skin of all thirty-two teeth

And then I shine my thirty-two some more…
And I smile myself right over a bush,
Tumbling
Head-first
Into a mess of –
Mud
And leaves
And –
Oh my gosh
That better not be shit…
–

I assess the damage
My jeans are wet with
Something
Mud decorating them…
I wonder if I could maybe get away with it –
Pass them off as some
New
Expensive
Denim
Wash
That only people who are
'really into fashion' would've heard of…
But then I look at my shirt
My shirt that now looks like Peppa Pig went
jumping all over it.
Nah, man!
And it's torn up, too!
And then
As if things couldn't get any worse…
I look down
And see that my
Fresh
White
Wedding
Air Forces
Are
White
No
More.

Beat.

This might be the worst day of my life.
–

The guys are gone now
And I don't know,
I might've preferred it if they just took me…
At least
Then
I'd have fresh creps
To be buried in.

Beat.

I get up.
Dust myself off.
And look around at the stretch of green before me.
'Cause I noticed my surroundings started looking
less familiar –
A while ago

BRIANNA   And I say less familiar,
Like I even knew where I was in the first place
'Cause, you know,
Directionally challenged and tings…
But at some point while I was taking pictures,
Things started looking a bit less like the park
And more like…
The woods,
Which is the last place a Black person should be,
to be honest
Like,
I didn't even go on my school's annual camping trip
'Cause I was that serious
About not 'disappearing under mysterious
circumstances'…
–

I flick through my camera roll,
Trying to pinpoint the exact moment
Where I obviously strayed from the path a bit,
And I can't lie,
I'm a sick photographer like…
You'd think this camera was magic, for real…
But it's not the best… tracker.
And I'd be mad at myself for getting distracted

But I kind of needed that…
That time.
Like therapy
while I'm on the NHS waiting list.
And the sun's been doing its thing with drying my
clothes…
Even if they are leaving some water marks behind.

AMANI   After a while
I check my phone
And
Google Maps tells me
I ran to the edge of Camberwell
That it's another forty-minute walk back to ends.
An hour if you count the walk to the right side of
Burgess Park.
My best bet? The Overground back to Peckham
But it's long either way.
And who is affording Uber in this economy??
(*Kisses teeth.*)
If I wasn't gonna be late before…
I'm defo late now.
Plus,
With the train times looking like they do:
Strikes –
I won't even have time to go home and change.
I flick back to the picture of Brianna
And I sigh.
Maybe
Maybe it's not a today ting.
Maybe…
It's not even you I'm chasing.

BRIANNA   As I'm walking,
I think about what I'm even gonna say to him
When we meet.
How I'm even gonna say it.
How I'm even gonna play it
'Cause I'm pretty by the script
I never freestyle
But something about this feels worthwhile…
I think…

I think Leema and KB would be proud of me
That I'm even here
Not just here as in, on my way to a real date,
But also here as in, wherever I am right now.

AMANI   I start the
Treacherous
Journey
Back.
Vigilant.
Just in case
Thing One
And
Thing Two
Are hiding in the shadows somewhere…

BRIANNA   After ten minutes pass,
I consider the
Teeny
Weeny
Minute
Possibility
That I might be lost.
Key word: consider.
'Cause if I acknowledge it fully…
Forget those grounding techniques,
I WILL be freaking out today.
See,
Google Maps is meant to be my friend, yeah,
But that little arrow stopped moving time ago,
Probably around the same time I finally lost my
last bar of reception…
Welp.
I think back to my friends
And decide that I WILL find my way out,
By fire or by force!
Now, I don't have the craziest survival skills ever
But I've watched enough wildlife programmes to
know just what I might be dealing with here…
I can't lie, though
If it wasn't still super bright outside,
It would be giving horror movie…

And we all know what happens to us lot in horror
movies…

Beat.

Nah, 'cause,
Who actually told me to do this?
Like,
I know I said I was on a 'saying yes' thing
But the woods????
I MUST be mad.
I think about my mum earlier,
And how she was trying her hardest to keep me
inside,
And how she might have been onto something,
actually
Because I might not ever see her,
Or Aliyah,
Or Nevaeh,
Again…
What?
Even though I'm convinced my mum found them
in a bin somewhere
In the seventh circle of hell –
Especially Aliyah –
I'd be lying if I said I wouldn't miss them…
And then I think about my friends,
Esther and Jess,
Who I met in halls,
Who I've been inseparable from ever since,
And who I'll probably never see again either…
Even Leema and KB,
Who might even be a bit responsible
'Cause this was even their idea in the first place
like…
And then I think about Amani,
Who'll probably think I stood him up or
something
When I'm actually
In a ditch somewhere
Getting nyam up by bears.
I can already see the headlines…

RIP me, man.
—
I take the time to just
Scream a bit.
I mean,
It fits the situation, and I've been needing to let off
some real steam since morning.
I just
Keep screaming.
Over
And over
Again.
Trying to empty myself
Of all the
Frustration
Pent up
From today.
And I guess it disturbs some birds
Who, unbeknownst to me, had been chilling on
a branch above my head…
I hear their wings catch the wind as they
frantically take off
In an attempt to escape the noise which ricochets
off of the trees in an echo that would inspire
a completely different atmosphere at night…
I hear their calls,
Desperate and dissipating…
And then I hear a
Splat.
And again.
Splat.
And then I feel them.
Both.
At once.
One right on my head,
As if my hair situation couldn't get any worse…
And the other on my left shoulder…
I scream again
But louder.
—
But then I hear the

CruuuunnNNNNCHHHH
Of footsteps
A shift in the wild
I feel the air change around me as the threat
Behind me lingers
Scramble for my house keys
Stick one between each finger
Ready my lungs 'cause I'm about to turn into
a singer and
I brace myself
'Cause this is probably the part in the movie
where I die
This is the real world my mum warned of come
alive
And what was I even thinking?? That the universe
would let me try??
I –
(*Man. Cockney accent.*) 'What are you doing?'
–

I look up,
Startled
'Uh uh I – '
(*Man.*) 'I'm not trying to hurt you, love… I asked
what you were doing.'
'Uhhhhh… Screaming?'
(*Man.*) 'Well, can you not? I'm tryna walk my dog
here.'
And sure enough,
A Labrador-looking thing comes running up to him,
Panting in the heat.
My eyes dart between him and the dog
And I pocket my keys slowly.
'Sorry. I just got pooed on.'
(*Man.*) 'I don't know why you're screaming for
then. Ain't that lucky?'
I tell him that I don't feel very lucky right now,
And before I even go down the route of
Trauma dumping on a literal stranger,
He says,
(*Man.*) 'You never know. Maybe something really
good is waiting for you.'

—

I think about Amani
And how I really hope that
He'll be that 'something good'…
'Yeah, maybe.'

Beat.

I apologise again for the disturbance, and he
points me back in the direction of the park,
unaware that he's just literally saved my life.

***

AMANI   See,
It must be talent…
'Cause the way I got back with –
Hmmm –
Two minutes to spare –
Yeah.
Looks like I
Still got some of that
'spirit of Usain' in me.
Not running away
But
Towards
A new finish line.

BRIANNA   When I finally find
Civilisation
Through a gap in some trees…
I actually think about what my life is right now.
It's saying ten minutes to the station
But I don't even wanna check how late I'm gonna
be to this date
That I honestly didn't even wanna go on in the
first place
That I've committed to…
'Cause it's all I've got to look forward to now…

AMANI   And yeah,
Maybe I should care more
But I've been through this much
And maybe she'll appreciate the effort.

BRIANNA   Maybe he'll admire my
          Strength
          Through all the
          trials
          And
          Tribulations

BOTH   Maybe it'll be a story we'll tell our kids.

BRIANNA   Or maybe
          I can just call it a day
          Go home
          And clean off all this bird shit.
          I don't know.

AMANI   'Cause I was banking on the low lighting masking
          all of these
          Fucking
          Stains but
          God, this is *so* bad.
          But the only issue,
          Aside from how much of a mess I look

BRIANNA   Is
          Not missing my train.

BOTH   I start running

AMANI   Sprinting

BRIANNA   Speeding
          Against the wind

AMANI   And then my head
          Suddenly feels cold
          A bit
          breezy
          In the
          Forehead region
          Which I don't really think about
          'Cause all I need to do right now is

BOTH   Catch
          That
          Train!

BRIANNA   I hear the call
          Echo
          Ringing
          Of the tannoy
          As it reads out my destination for the last time.

BOTH   Catch
          That
          Train!

AMANI   I hear the ding
          Dong
          Pinging
          Of the doors as they warn me.

BOTH   Catch
          That
          Train!

BRIANNA   I hear the
          Creaking
          Sliding
          Scraping
          Of the doors on the closest carriage as they shut.

BOTH   Catch
          That
          Train!

AMANI   I hear the turning
          Rolling
          Twisting
          Of wheels
          As the train starts
          Centimetre
          Millimetre
          Inching
          Forward.
          Taunting me.

BOTH   I've missed it.

          Beat.

          I've missed it.

***

AMANI   Two youngish
           Secondary school-looking girls watch me from
           a carriage window
           Taunting me too.
           And they keep –
           They keep pointing at –
           They're pointing at my head!
           My hand flies up
           And lands
           On my cranium.
           My
           Bare
           Cranium.
           My
           Exposed
           cranium.
           My
           Durag-less
           Cranium.
           No.
           No no no
           'Cause that means…
           That means…
           I trace the wonky line
           That Junior carved into my curls
           And remember.

           Beat.

           The girls,
           Realising
           That I've finally realised
           Start laughing their heads off
           As the train fully departs.

BRIANNA   See,
           I was hoping to catch the Windrush back to
           familiar lands…
           but
           Just as I'm about to
           Maybe

Go against my better judgement
A group of kids walk past me with their phones
out.
Laughing.
Saying something about me looking a mess,
Something about the shit in my hair and across my
shoulder and back…
And usually it wouldn't get to me,
But the day's already been beating me up so
like…
Just 'low me, innit.
'Yeah well… your mum!' I shout back,
'And bird poo is actually lucky… actually, so
there!'

—

Okayyyy
So it's been a while since I've had to cuss out year
sevens!

—

But it's also like…
They're right.

—

I look down at myself again

AMANI   And I can't lie…
             Fuck this.
             Next train's in… what?
             Twenty minutes?
             The Overground times are better,
             But no way I'm making six.
             No way I'm going.
             'Cause between
             Missing my trim appointment
             'Cause my nan couldn't work the TV,

BRIANNA   Between my sisters stealing my clothes
             And ruining them,

AMANI   / Letting the demon barber Junior
             Massacre
             My hairline
             And having my friends take the absolute piss,

> Getting chased down
> And almost jumped
> By two wastemen by a bus stop
> And running into a bush,
> Missing my train…

BRIANNA   / My mum holding me hostage with housework,
Getting soaked by those kids outside of Annie's
Getting lost in the woods,
And then SHAT on by some
DUTTY.
STINKING.
PIGEONS.
And getting laughed at by some yutes…

BOTH   I don't even know why I'm still here.

AMANI   This whole time,
I've been tryna
Stay positive…
Excited…
'Cause at least I get to meet
'Her'.

BRIANNA   Tryna really put myself out there FOR ONCE!
But to be honest,

AMANI   / I don't even know the girl.

BRIANNA   / I don't even know the guy

AMANI   And there have been NUFF signs!
Like –

BOTH   All I had to do was get from A to B
In one piece.

BRIANNA   And I couldn't even do that.

AMANI   I'm actually kind of wondering if I
killed someone in my past life or something???
'Cause what in the bad karma *is* this???

Beat.

I pick up my phone –

BRIANNA   And dial for Leema.

AMANI   And dial for KB.

BRIANNA   It only rings –

AMANI   Twice
           Before he picks up.
           All –

BRIANNA   Cheery like –

AMANI   (*Leema.*) 'Omg, hey! Don't tell me you lot are
           together?! I'm gonna get K – '

BRIANNA   'Yeahhh about that, Leems…'

AMANI   'I can't make it.'

BRIANNA   (*KB.*) 'What do you mean, you can't make it?'

AMANI   'I mean… I'm really sorry. Tell Leems I'm sorry,
           too.'

BRIANNA   'I know you really wanted this to happen.
           For us to meet – '

AMANI   'But K, if you knew what kind of day I've had…'

BRIANNA   (*KB.*) 'Your date said the same thing, so what?'

AMANI   'So… Maybe it's a sign.'

BRIANNA   'Some things just aren't meant to be, you know.'

AMANI   (*Leema.*) 'If you think I'm gonna let you sack it
           off just 'cause you've had a bit of a bad day – '

BRIANNA   'Nah you don't understand…
           It hasn't just been bad – '

AMANI   'It's been absolutely – '

BRIANNA   'Unequivocally – '

BOTH   'Shit.'

BRIANNA   'And I honestly just wanna go home.
           So maybe next time, yeah?'

AMANI   He sighs.
           And I can sense his disappointment

BRIANNA   Right through the phone.
            Then Leema goes,

AMANI   (*Leema*.) 'I think you're making a mistake.
            I think…
            I think it would've been so worth it.
            For you guys to finally meet.
            If not for each other,
            Then for yourselves.'
            And I say,

BRIANNA   'Yeah.'

AMANI   'Maybe.'

BOTH   I look at the picture in my phone again

AMANI   And I think about how
            I must've thought she was worth it.
            Worth the risk of being seen
            I mean,
            I was about to show up
            On a date
            Covered in dirt
            With an absolutely tragic excuse for a line-up
            Almost an hour late…
            And I don't know…

BRIANNA   Maybe the universe is just… moving mad.
            Telling me that it's not the day, or he's not the one.

AMANI   But maybe it's asking me –

BRIANNA   'How bad do you want this?'

AMANI   'Cause nothing worthwhile comes easy, right?
            I hear my dad in my head and he's saying
            'After the day you've had? You've earned it.'
            But deep down,
            I don't really know if –

BRIANNA   I *deserve* it.

AMANI   'Cause it's been a while since even *I* have looked
            below my surface

What if she does
And decides I'm not worth it?

Beat.

But then again…

BOTH   What if we're just… perfect?

BRIANNA   If I wait for 'next time' to be THEE time, is it ever
gonna come?
I'm staring 'New Brianna' in the face
And she's saying, 'this is it'.

AMANI   'Suck it up.'

BRIANNA   And I start to feel this pressing weight the size of
Mum's words lift…
Because it's *me* that gets to choose this.

BOTH   Fuck it.

Beat.

AMANI   I've gotta meet her.

BOTH   My train comes

AMANI   The wheels screech as it
Grinds
To a halt
I get on,
And I choose the front carriage
'Cause I see a man with a friendly face
And I need that right now.

BRIANNA   I'm still deep in thought as I push myself through
the sliding doors
Still not really sure
Kinda
Zombified.
Some people stare,
'Cause I look kind of mad right now –

AMANI   Probably smell kind of mad right now
And people can't just mind their business –

BRIANNA   I fiddle with my camera strap
           Ready to recount my journey through pictures

AMANI   Tuck my notebook under my arm
           'Cause I know I've got some feels to get out

BRIANNA   I make my way down the carriage
           Take my seat

AMANI   Staying clear of the windows

BRIANNA   Head down

AMANI   Floating

BOTH   Trying my best
           Not to be seen
           And –

They both stop before each other, looking up for the first time since they got on the train. Their worlds are fully merged for the first time.

BRIANNA looks first, checking if it's the person in the picture.
AMANI does a double take.
Their eyes meet.
And they kind of point
In disbelief.

AMANI   Brianna?

BRIANNA   Amani

For a moment they just sit there, scanning each other.

BRIANNA tucks her camera behind her and AMANI does the same with his notebook. And then they laugh. And laugh again, because of course it was always going to happen like this.

BOTH   Hi.

End.

A Nick Hern Book

A to B first published in Great Britain in 2026 as a paperback original by
Nick Hern Books Limited, The Glasshouse, 49a Goldhawk Road, London W12 8QP, in
association with JFR Productions, HighTide Theatre and Soho Theatre, London

A to B copyright © 2026 Tia-Renee Mullings

Tia-Renee Mullings has asserted her moral right to be identified as the author of
this work

Cover photograph by Courtney Nathan Phillip; post-production edit by
David Oldenburg

Designed and typeset by Nick Hern Books, London
Printed in the UK by Mimeo Ltd, Huntingdon, Cambridgeshire PE29 6XX

A CIP catalogue record for this book is available from the British Library

ISBN 978 1 83904 575 2

www.nickhernbooks.co.uk/environmental-policy

Nick Hern Books' authorised representative in the EU is
Easy Access System Europe – Mustamäe tee 50, 10621 Tallinn, Estonia
email gpsr.requests@easproject.com